I0413564

101

Inspirational Quotes

Volume 1

Compiled by

Séamus Martin

Published 2014 by Séamus Martin

Copyright © Séamus Martin 2014

ISBN-13: 978-1495901690

ISBN-10: 1495901696

Categories:

Reference – Quotations

For Sinéad.

Introduction

> As a single footstep will not make a path on the earth, so a single thought will not make a pathway in the mind.
>
> To make a deep physical path, we walk again and again.
>
> To make a deep mental path, we must think over and over the kind of thoughts we wish to dominate our lives.
>
> - Henry David Thoreau

Are you in need of an emotional shot-in-the-arm?

I know I certainly was. I had lost my voice and was going through the wringer with a viral illness. Physically drained and mentally miserable, with only Facebook for company, I found myself clicking on a photo of an inspirational quotation that someone had posted. Then another and another.

Pretty soon I started feeling happier. And some of the quotations I actually found very thought-provoking, inspiring and challenging. Before I knew it, I was feeling much more positive on many levels and found myself thinking long and hard about my life and my future.

I started typing up a list of the quotations which I found most helpful and so that I could refer to them again and again all in one place. Then I started looking for additional pearls of wisdom, and soon I had a collection of dozens, scores, over a hundred quotations. They are proving a great source of motivation to me and have inspired me to take action to improve my situation.

I came to realise that surely other people's lives could also be made better and happier through these quotations, and that it would be wrong of me to hide this light under a bushel. And so now here in this book are the inspirational sayings I have collected- shared with the world and shared with you.

Enjoy.

And be inspired to take action!

Séamus Martin

February 2014

PS   Despite my best efforts, I have been unable to track down the original source of some of these quotations, and they therefore appear as "unknown". I would be grateful for any information regarding who said these first so that I may correctly attribute these quotes in the next edition of this book.

1

You cannot open a book without learning something.

— Confucius

2

Rules for Happiness:

Something to do,

Someone to love,

Something to hope for.

- Immanuel Kant

3

You can have everything in life you want, if you will just help other people get what they want.

- Zig Ziglar

4

Watch your thoughts;
they become words.

Watch your words;
they become actions.

Watch your actions;
they become habits.

Watch your habits;
they become character.

Watch your character;
it becomes your destiny.

- Frank Outlaw

5

You're off to great places!

Today is your day!

Your mountain is waiting,

So... get on your way!

- Dr. Seuss
Oh, the Places You'll Go!

6

"It's impossible," said Pride.

"It's risky," said Experience.

"It's pointless," said Reason.

"Give it a try," whispered the Heart.

   - Unknown

7

There are only two mistakes you can make along the road to truth:

Not going all the way,

And not getting started.

- Buddha

8

Life feels better when you have a plan.

– Advertising slogan of the *Scottish Widows* pensions and investments company

Whatever you can do or dream you can, begin it.

Boldness has genius, power and magic in it!

-Johann Wolfgang von Goethe

10

You can't calm the storm…
so stop trying.

What you can do is calm yourself.

The storm will pass.

   - Timber Hawkeye

11

Do.

Or do not.

There is no try!

   - Yoda
   Star Wars

Failure should be our teacher, not our undertaker.

Failure is delay, not defeat.

It is a temporary detour, not a dead end.

Failure is something we can avoid only by:

Saying nothing,

Doing nothing

And being nothing.

- Denis Waitley

13

Take the first chance that you get because you may never get another one.

 – Unknown

Instead of asking what the world needs, ask what makes you come alive, and go do it. Because what the world needs is people who have come alive.

- Howard Thurman

15

Many of us are afraid to follow our passions, to pursue what we want most because it means taking risks and even facing failure.

But to pursue your passion with all your heart and soul is success in itself.

The greatest failure is to have never really tried.

– Robyn Allan

I do it because I can.

I can because I want to.

I want to...

Because you said I couldn't!

   - Unknown

17

Do not let your fire go out, spark by irreplaceable spark in the hopeless swamps of the not-quite, the not-yet, and the not-at-all.

Do not let the hero in your soul perish in lonely frustration for the life you deserved and have never been able to reach.

The world you desire can be won.

It exists. It is real. It is possible.

It's yours!

- Ayn Rand, *Atlas Shrugged*

When I was 5 years old, my mother always told me that happiness was the key to life.

When I went to school, they asked me what I wanted to be when I grew up.

I wrote down 'happy'.

They told me I didn't understand the assignment.

I told them they didn't understand life.

- John Lennon

I am not sure exactly what heaven will be like, but I know that when we die and it comes time for God to judge us, he will not ask,

'How many good things have you done in your life?'

Rather he will ask,

'How much love did you put into what you did?

   - Mother Teresa

20

Every time I thought I was being rejected from something good, I was actually being redirected to something better.

– Dr. Steve Maraboli

Respect yourself enough to walk away from anything that no longer serves you, grows you, or makes you happy.

If you aren't being treated with love and respect, check your price tag. Maybe you've marked yourself down.

It's YOU who tells people what you're worth.

Get off of the clearance rack and get behind the glass where they keep the valuables.

– Robert Tew

Worry is worthless.

Worry is thinking about everything that has gone wrong, is going wrong, and will go wrong.

To worry about what you can't change is useless.

To worry about what you can change is a waste of time.

Either change it or forget it!

– Dr. Alan Zimmerman

23

There is nothing wrong with dreaming big dreams.

Just know that all roads that lead to success have to pass through *Hard Work Boulevard* at some point.

- Eric Thomas

24

May your choices reflect your hopes, not your fears.

– Nelson Mandela

25

Happiness is not something ready-made. It comes from your own actions.

- Dalai Lama

26

Ask yourself if what you are doing today is getting you closer to where you want to be tomorrow.

– Unknown

27

A smile is a curve that sets everything straight.

– Phyllis Diller

28

If you are always trying to be normal, you will never know how amazing you can be!

- Maya Angelou

You never learn when things are going smoothly.

– Virginia Satir

30

The grass is greener...

Where you water it!

– Neil Barringham

31

Good habits are as addictive as bad habits, and a lot more rewarding!

– Harvey Mackay

32

If beating yourself up worked, you'd be rich, thin, and happy.

Try loving yourself instead.

– Cheryl Richardson

33

People are rewarded in public for what they practice for years in private.

- Anthony Robbins

34

A word of encouragement during a failure is worth more than an hour of praise after success.

– Unknown.

35

Two of the hardest tests in life:

The patience to wait for the right moment

And courage to accept whatever you encounter.

– Paulo Coelho

When something goes wrong in your life,

just yell 'plot twist!'

and then move on.

– Unknown

37

Life isn't about waiting for the storm to pass.

It's about learning to dance in the rain.

- Vivian Greene

38

Whatever you are,

Be a good one.

   - Abraham Lincoln

39

You are never too old to re-invent yourself.

- Steve Harvey

Always be a first-rate version of yourself, instead of a second-rate version of somebody else.

- Judy Garland

41

Do what you feel in your heart to be right. For you'll be criticized anyway.

- Eleanor Roosevelt

42

In the end, it's not going to matter how many breaths you took, but how many moments took your breath away.

- Shing Xiong

Be who you are and say what you feel because those who mind don't matter and those who matter don't mind.

- Dr. Seuss

44

Our greatest glory is not in never falling, but in rising every time we fall.

– Confucius

45

People with clear, written goals, accomplish far more in a shorter period of time than people without them could ever imagine.

– Brian Tracy

46

When you feel like giving up, remember why you held on for so long in the first place.

– Unknown

47

Don't judge each day by the harvest you reap but by the seeds that you plant.

- Robert Louis Stevenson

When one door closes, another opens; but we often look so long and so regretfully upon the closed door that we do not see the one that has opened for us.

- Helen Keller

49

Work like you don't need the money,

Love like you've never been hurt

And dance like no one is watching.

   - Randall G Leighton

If you don't like something,
change it.

If you can't change it,
change your attitude.

Don't complain.

- Maya Angelou

Nothing worthwhile comes easily. Work, continuous work and hard work, is the only way to accomplish results that last.

- Hamilton Holt

You are free to choose,

But you are not free to alter the consequences of your decisions.

- Ezra Taft Benson

53

It's not about where you're from.
It's all about where you're going.

– Randy Gage

54

There comes a point in your life
when you realise

Who really matters,

Who never did,

And who always will.

   – Unknown

55

If you love someone tell them...
because hearts are often broken
by words left unspoken.

- Pamela Daranjo

56

Wherever you are, be all there.

- Jim Elliot

57

Peace begins with a smile.

- Mother Teresa

Three-fourths of the people you will ever meet are hungering and thirsting for sympathy. Give it to them, and they will love you.

- Dale Carnegie

Sometimes our light goes out, but is blown again into instant flame by an encounter with another human being.

- Albert Schweitzer

You can't stay in your corner of the forest waiting for others to come to you. You have to go to them sometimes.

- A.A. Milne
Winnie-the-Pooh

If you go looking for a friend, you're going to find they're very scarce.

If you go out to be a friend, you'll find them everywhere.

- Zig Ziglar

Nobody wakes up happy and successful.

You must first decide that you truly, deep down, want to be happier and more successful.

It isn't something you fall into.

It starts with a decision you make.

— Dr. Alan Zimmerman

63

The important risks you don't take today will become tomorrow's regrets.

- Unknown

64

Turn your wounds into wisdom.

- Oprah Winfrey

Courage is not the absence of fear, but rather the judgement that something else is more important than fear.

- Ambrose Redmoon

66

It's not whether you fail or not. It's how you respond when it happens.

– Robert Kiyosaki

Passion – vigorous enthusiasm – always trumps excuses.

- Dr. Wayne W. Dyer

68

The mind is its own place,

And in itself can make a heaven of hell,

A hell of heaven.

- John Milton
Paradise Lost

You never fail until you stop trying.

- Albert Einstein

Life isn't about finding yourself.

Life is about creating yourself!

- George Bernard Shaw

The things you are passionate about are not random. They are your calling.

- Fabienne Fredrickson

72

Always do what you are afraid to do.

- Ralph Waldo Emerson

73

And, when you want something, all the universe conspires in helping you to achieve it.

-Paulo Coelho

74

Give thanks for unknown
blessings already on their way.

- Native American saying

The only way to make sense out of change is to plunge into it, move with it, and join the dance.

- Alan Watts

Nothing is impossible.

The word itself says

"I'm possible"!

   - Audrey Hepburn

Anything's possible if you've got enough nerve.

- J.K. Rowling
Harry Potter and the Half-Blood Prince

78

Only in the darkness can you see the stars.

- Martin Luther King Jr.

79

Don't worry about those who talk behind your back. They're behind you for a reason.

— Unknown

The greatest prison that people live in is the fear of what other people think.

- David Icke

Reputation is what other people know about you.

Honour is what you know about yourself.

- Lois McMaster Bujold

82

What's the good of living if you don't try a few things?

- Charles M. Schulz

Those who move forward with a happy spirit will find that things always work out.

- Gordon B. Hinckley

A ship is safe in harbour, but that's not what ships are for.

- William G.T. Shedd

85

One does not discover new lands without consenting to lose sight of the shore for a very long time.

- Andre Gide

86

The first step toward getting somewhere is to decide that you are not going to stay where you are.

- John Pierpont Morgan

87

I can only show you the door.

You're the one who has to walk through it.

- Morpheous
The Matrix

What's terrible is to pretend that second-rate is first-rate.

To pretend that you don't need love when you do;

Or you like your work when you know quite well you're capable of better.

- Doris Lessing
The Golden Notebook

89

The things you do for yourself are gone when you are gone, but the things you do for others remain as your legacy.

- Kalu Ndukwe Kalu

The secret to your future is in your daily routine.

If you want anything great, it will come out of a whole host of small things that you do on a regular basis.

Change involves discipline.

– Dr. Alan Zimmerman

91

Don't cry because it is over.

Smile because it happened!

- Gabriel Garcia Marquez

92

Everything is okay in the end.

If it's not ok,

Then it's not the end.

 – Unknown

Why are you trying so hard to fit in when you were born to stand out?

- From the film *What A Girl Wants*

94

He who is not courageous enough to take risks will accomplish nothing in life.

– Muhammad Ali

95

Anyone can hide. Facing up to things, working through them, that's what makes you strong.

- Sarah Dessen

96

Yesterday you said 'tomorrow'.

– Nike advert

It's not what you are that holds you back,

It's what you think you are not.

- Denis Waitley

98

A year from now you may wish you had started today!

- Karen Lamb

Isn't it nice to think that tomorrow is a new day with no mistakes in it yet?

- L.M. Montgomery

100

For attractive lips,
speak words of kindness.

For lovely eyes,
seek out the good in people.

For a slim figure,
share your food with the hungry.

For beautiful hair,
let a child run their fingers
through it once a day.

For poise,
walk with the knowledge that
you never walk alone.

People, more than things, have to be restored, renewed, revived, reclaimed, and redeemed.

Remember, if you ever need a helping hand, you will find one at the end of each of your arms.

As you grow older, you will discover that you have two hands, one for helping yourself and the other for helping others.

- Sam Levenson

One evening an old Cherokee told his grandson about a debate that goes on inside people. He said,

"My son, the battle between two wolves is inside us all. One is Evil. It is anger, envy, jealousy, sorrow, regret, greed, arrogance, self-pity, guilt, resentment, inferiority, lies, false pride, superiority, and ego.

The other is good. It is joy, peace, love, hope, serenity, humility, kindness, benevolence, empathy, generosity, truth, compassion, and faith."

The grandson thought about this for a minute and then asked his grandfather:

"Which wolf wins?"

The old Cherokee simply replied,

"The one you feed."

- Native American story